NOT THE SONNETS

Other Books by Ian Gouge

Novels and Novellas

Tilt - Coverstory books, 2023
Once Significant Others - Coverstory books, 2023
On Parliament Hill - Coverstory books, 2021
A Pattern of Sorts - Coverstory books, 2020
The Opposite of Remembering - Coverstory books, 2020
At Maunston Quay - Coverstory books, 2019
An Infinity of Mirrors - Coverstory books, 2018 (2nd ed.)
The Big Frog Theory - Coverstory books, 2018 (2nd ed.)
Losing Moby Dick and Other Stories - Coverstory books, 2017

Short Stories

An Irregular Piece of Sky - Coverstory books, 2023
Degrees of Separation - Coverstory books, 2018
Secrets & Wisdom - Paperback, 2017

Poetry

Crash - Coverstory books, 2023
not the Sonnets - Coverstory books, 2023
Selected Poems: 1976-2022 - Coverstory books, 2022
The Homelessness of a Child - Coverstory books, 2021
The Myths of Native Trees - Coverstory books, 2020
First-time Visions of Earth from Space - Coverstory books, 2019
After the Rehearsals - Coverstory books, 2018
Punctuations from History - Coverstory books, 2018
Human Archaeology - Paperback, 2017
Collected Poems (1979-2016) - KDP, 2017

Non-Fiction

Shrapnel from a Writing Life - Coverstory books, 2022

IAN GOUGE

NOT THE SONNETS

First published in paperback format by Coverstory books, 2023

ISBN 978-1-7397660-3-0 (paperback)

Copyright © Ian Gouge 2023

The right of Ian Gouge to be identified as the author of this work has been asserted by him in accordance with the Copyright, Designs and Patents Act 1988.

All characters and events in this publication. other than those clearly in the public domain, are fictitious and any resemblance to real persons, living or dead, is purely coincidental.

The cover image was designed by the author © Ian Gouge 2023

All rights reserved.

No part of this publication may be reproduced, circulated, stored in a system from which it can be retrieved, or transmitted in any form without the prior permission in writing of the publisher.

www.iangouge.com

www.coverstorybooks.com

for Elizabeth Barraclough -
who didn't much care for
poetry that failed to rhyme…

Contents

Foreword 1	The Would-be Poet (as a young man) 45
On Being Thrown Over 5	Eulogy 46
January Chill 6	Looking Back from Catbells 47
Obituary of a Would-be Poet 7	When he chose not to go 48
The Generous and the Selfish 8	Weather Report 49
Abandoned 9	Battle of the Sexes 50
In Search of Tabloid Headlines 10	Between the Pear and the Cheese 51
Pilgrimage 11	Brain-washing 52
In the Hospice 12	Love's impossible equation 53
In Mourning 13	Mourning those things I didn't know I'd miss 54
On Being Asked To Prove Love 14	The Hare become the Tortoise 55
Unrequited Love 15	"The Magpie" 56
Defenceless Against Time 16	A Kind of Dorian Grey 57
Orienteering 17	Ageing Ungracefully 58
On Not Accepting Your Faith In The Stars ... 18	Heritage 59
Fearing Dementia 19	A Casanova's Main Course 60
The Claims You Made 20	Dante's Muse Speaks 61
Conversation With My Muse 21	Stockholm Syndrome 62
Frost & Fog 22	Snapshot in the Institution's Garden 63
Constructive Criticism 23	On the Isthmus 64
Compulsion 24	Insomnia 65
The Shakespearian Lead 25	Lonely Hearts Ad 66
New Moon, Old Anguish 26	Gawain's Farewell 67
Moving On 27	"Baz Woz 'Ere" 68
Slam, Vulnerable 28	Elizabethan 69
Undercover Writer 29	Remembering Authenticity 70
Falling Apart 30	Mining for Truth 71
Perspective 31	An Optimist Falls Into March 72
Heading into Winter 32	On the Red Carpet 73
Camelot's Phoenix 33	Tea and scones for two? 74
Reparations 34	And so I 75
Heart-to-heart 35	No way back 76
In Which She Mocks His Romanticism 36	The Song of the Poet in Political Exile - I 77
Comeuppance: Reality TV 37	The Song of the Poet in Political Exile - II 78
Eulogy for a Villain 38	On White Scar 79
Mirror-talk 39	Blah, blah, blah 80
Judgement Day (aged 16, 18, 21…) 40	Subject Matter: Memoir 81
Me, v9.0 41	Pickpocket of Plagiarism 82
Première 42	Dancing to the Tune 83
Castaway 43	A Farewell Letter 84
The Inevitable Covid Poem 44	Recipe 85

Pen-portraits 86	The Manifesto of the Soul..............................129
Balance Sheet 87	The Terror of Clock Chimes 130
The Magician's Would-be Biographers...........88	Slave Trader...131
"you leave something of yourself in the marks you make" 89	A Game of Chance 132
	Descent thru' Virtue and Vice 133
Mining Memory 90	Seashore Sunset...134
Ambition Misaligned..91	5-right; 58-left..135
Lancelot, on leaving Camelot..........................92	Mourning Clothes 136
Methods of Self-Defence 93	One more day in Confinement......................137
After the Interview 94	Song of the Abused 138
A Gambler's Faith 95	The Beneficiary 139
I did not see her leave......................................96	Waiting for a train, nervously........................140
History in a Packing-Case 97	Catch, landed...141
On taking on an allotment 98	Young and Old Revolutionaries in Conversation..142
Politic's Greasy Pole, July 2022 - I 99	
Politic's Greasy Pole, July 2022 - II.............100	Testimony of a War Artist..............................143
Politic's Greasy Pole, July 2022 - III 101	Opening the Bowling 144
The Green Man 102	Bitter Harvest 145
The Coming of Winter 103	Second Among Equals 146
Miners Greeting the Dawn...........................104	The Great Escape 147
Sifting through the Sand...............................105	Treasure Island..148
From the edge of the meadow......................106	At the Un-fun Fair 149
Writer-in-residence 107	Fracking Greed 150
In an Italian Cathedral 108	Residue from an Argument............................151
Free Will 109	As the Incompetents hog the Stage 152
Banquo's Ghost on The Witches 110	After I won the Lottery...................................153
Similarities between Politicians & Poets.......111	Over-reaction to a Ill-timed Accusation........154
Curtain Call? 112	The Friar Protests 155
From the trenches...113	Blind Loyalty 156
Valentine 114	Bottom's Bully-boy..157
The Rechargeable Battery 115	Dreaming of Daggers......................................158
"A Dummy's Guide to Imposter Syndrome" 116	Acknowledgements 161
Monsters in the Dark 117	
Viewers' Vote 118	
The Toss of a Coin..119	
On Once Requited Love 120	
At the Garden Gate..121	
Watching You Sleep..122	
Olympic Redemption 123	
Scars from a Mugging....................................124	
The Hunt for Meaning in Experience 125	
Check-up...126	
On revisiting an old home now derelict 127	
Industrial Unrest 128	

x

Foreword

There is a 'scene' in my verse narrative, *After the Rehearsals*, where the lead character gives a poetic eulogy at his sister's funeral. It is, I suppose, a *Stop All The Clocks* moment[1], and so - even though the piece in *After the Rehearsals* is wholly mine - from the perspective of the 'filmic' insertion, the notion itself is not entirely original. When I came to write the eulogy I tried to think how someone who was not 'a writer' might embark on such an onerous task, and settled on a reworking of one of Shakespeare's sonnets. Why would they not start using the building blocks of something known, exceptional, proven? Obviously my character would be changing the meaning of the piece, but in terms of approach, style, emotion and 'feel', it seemed the right thing to do. So appropriate, in fact, that I did it twice in the same book!

Setting aside any considerations relating to the quality of the final output, undertaking the 'reworking' of a Shakespearean sonnet was, above anything else, a challenge. If the final pieces in *After the Rehearsals* are not as 'perfect' as I might wish them to be, as a result they are potentially even *more* fitting for the character who has crafted them as he is no poet. I think they work well enough within the context of that narrative, so job done.

A fellow writer, on hearing the piece in isolation, wondered if I hadn't somehow straight-jacketed myself; or even if the task was doomed to failure because of its source. And they may have had a point. Forcing myself to adhere - more or less - to the rhythmical form (though not necessarily the meter), perhaps those two efforts came across as a tad 'forced', a little dated. However, given their context and nominal 'author', this was fine; they were serving their narrative purpose.

---

[1] A reference to the use of W H Auden's poem, *Twelve Songs (ix)* - now popularly known as *Stop All The Clocks* - in the Richard Curtis film, "Four Weddings and a Funeral".

It was probably at the point of completing *After the Rehearsals* that the idea of tackling the entirety of Shakespeare's sonnet cannon in a similar vein came to me: would it be possible to 're-imagine' all 154 of *The Sonnets*, to give them a new twist, to make them contemporary and modern, to at least partially free them from their time-honoured love-bound context? And if so, how?

Initially at least, it was an experiment. I decided to start where most poets end i.e. with the rhyme. I began by stripping out every single word from each of the poems except the last one on each line. This had been the approach I had taken with the *After the Rehearsals* pieces, and it worked there - after a fashion, anyway! And, unless the subject of the new piece demanded it, I would allow myself the freedom *not* to stick to the sonnet's original subject. The last thing I wanted to produce was something that was little more than pastiche, a regurgitation of nearly thirteen dozen love poems! At all costs I needed to avoid saying the same thing over and over again, and/or in the same way; each poem needed to be able to stand on its own unmetered feet.

Of course the starting point - the chain of those last words - offered two immediate challenges. The first was the nature of the language itself (e.g. the considerable number of repetitions of 'thee', and the plethora of archaic words ending in 'est'). Setting out some loose rules, I decided to allow myself the latitude to amend or replace - but within the rhythmical confines of each sonnet. For example, in #3 'viewest' becomes 'view', 'renewest' becomes 'renew', and 'thee' becomes 'alchemy' (to keep the rhyme).

The second challenge was subject. It is with subject that most poems start, and if one is rhyming - to any schema - rhyme almost always comes last. By tackling the pieces so completely the other way around, the primary question became 'what subject will fit a poem whose lines end with these <u>exact</u> words?' Solving that particular conundrum is much harder than you might imagine! I found as I worked through each sonnet that the subject of my 'translation' often changed; I might start thinking it was a love poem (often inevitable, even though I wanted to avoid those as much as possible!) yet through rewriting, found it being transformed into something else entirely. When one starts with one's own draft words on the virgin page, there is something of you already invested in them before editing begins, an investment which can mean making wholesale changes particularly difficult: When you are starting with fourteen words that are absolutely *not* your own, every other word you subsequently put down on the page seems magically to become fair game. The degree of liberation is considerable.

Perhaps unsurprisingly, there was actually a third challenge; one which appeared soon after the first few poems were drafted. And that was the challenge of metre. If rhyme is the most common trap laid by the gods of pastiche, the second has to be rhythm. All the while the poems - the words in the poems - sat on the page arrayed in fourteen lines, rhyme screaming out at the end of each and every one of them, then instinct, conditioning (call it what you will) kicks in i.e. the writerly impulse to fall into some dum-de-dum-dum-de-dum meter, line after line. Make no mistake, it was not so much the words themselves beating this drum - though they had a significant role to play in it, of course - but rather how they *looked* which set expectations. And how could I *not* know their source was a Shakespearean sonnet in the first place? If the rhyme were the straitjacket, then the appearance of fourteen lines on the page fixed the buckles. Such a layout seemed to insist on syllable count. No, it *demanded* it.

In spite of a stated desire to diverge and modernise, it proved difficult not to give in to the compulsion to adopt ten syllables per line, and to beat a tattoo which proclaimed "this is a sonnet!" Only by physically breaking those bonds and by running lines together when drafting the poems (i.e. making them something other than 14-lines) was I able to loose myself Houdini-like.

And then something else interesting happened. As I began to draft more pieces in this prose-like layout, I found the original dominance of rhythm weakening, and then it became possible to once again see the poems as fourteen lines and not *feel* them as sonnets. The seventh was the first example of that. Not only did it work as a fourteen line poem and a piece where the rhyme was not a burden, I found that it stood on its own two feet well enough to be the first to be rewarded with a title. It became 'Pilgrimage'; it was no longer '#7'.

This was a breakthrough. It was as if I had discovered a new rhythm for the poems. It allowed me to revisit some of those that I had rough-hewn into coarse strings of words, and free them back into the fourteen line pattern from which they had originally sprung. The pastiche had been magically banished; it was now a new mythology, like seeing a swan emerge from an untidy and grubby cygnet. More than that. Knowing I could achieve my goal allowed me to go back to drafting some of the later sonnets from their original scaffolding -without falling into the original traps.

People will have their own views, of course. The upshot of all this theorising - never mind the fundamentals of the undertaking - may simply be to offer ammunition to those who feel the overall premise is profoundly 'wrong', that the audacity of stealing from the Bard is a capital offence. On that basis, my decision to call the collection *not the Sonnets* is one which aims to reflect the fact that, by and large, these pieces are something else entirely. Conversely, the title also tries to recognise the poems' source, and in the back-to-front endeavour of the whole thing, the denial of what they are (or are no longer) is perhaps only fitting.

Ian Gouge, 2023

On Being Thrown Over

Would your love for me increase
were I to die?
Barely-mourned, would my decease
erase me from your memory?

Just when did your febrile eyes
seek solace in others, find the fuel
to weave a quilt of lies
pre-posthumously cruel?

Was I no more than ornament,
a transient nod to Spring,
the blush of one short season's mild content
now only fit for fickle disregarding?

Was there nothing more I could ever be,
a dull fragment of your history?

January Chill

I no longer mind your troubled brow
naked like a frosted winter field.
I cannot soothe it now.

And if I see those hands no longer held
as slick ministers of your lies
I could remember summer days
when there was harvest in our eyes.

Neither vanity nor self-praise
drives my search for words to use
in recompense for what's no longer mine.
I forage without excuse
for sanctuary against the blizzard Time;
my only comfort when I'm frail and old
to stare down the triumph of your bitter cold.

Obituary of a Would-be Poet

Fettered by one uninspiring view
he sought another,
as if a fresh approach might renew
an imperfect translation of his mother
tongue. Verbal tricks sleight-handed since the womb
he attributed to genius for husbandry,
early-investments for a life beyond the tomb,
an embalming in linguistic posterity.

He thought words would set him free
and preserve him past his prime,
yet it was easy for the rest of us to see
his looming defeat to vengeful time;
that for all his ball-pen potions he would never be
a master of poetic alchemy.

The Generous and the Selfish

Fearing the disease, his vaccine was to spend,
giving as immunisation, a cellular legacy.
There was nothing he would not lend
as if philanthropy set him free.

Yet it failed to silence the abuse
from those who could not give,
those shackled by a primitive urge to steal, to use
and plunder and then to live
self-condemned, alone,
undone by an instinct to deceive.

There will be no fanfare when they have gone,
taken their slinking leave
defeated by philanthropy
and never knowing how it's best to be.

Abandoned

Beyond this warped picket frame
stands the derelict house where you no longer dwell;
unruly thistles jostle in that same
romantic spot where once we'd kiss and tell.
How can it be that you moved on
and chose not to take me there?
That the cradle of our love is gone
its varnish cracking crumbling everywhere?

Yet did I hear your whisper just as I left?
Catch your shadow in the fractured glass?

For an instant I was less bereft
buoyed by remembering what once was,
recalling how we used to meet
and taste the taste of us so sweet.

In Search of Tabloid Headlines

Will your ambition deface
our past and see our lives distilled
and paraded naked in this impersonal place?
More than my affection will be killed
by such crude self-serving usury.

Seduced by mythic income
you gamble recklessly
chasing prizes to out-strip everyone,
abandoning the old pretence that Love is Art.

How can I condone this calumny
and betrayal, your decision to depart
driven by cheap fame and weak posterity?
You hope judgement will be fair,
that legend - not notoriety - will be your heir.

Pilgrimage

We set off before first light
the pre-dawn drive straining the eye.
Numbed by pulsing headlights, my sight
tried to race ahead, to preview the majesty
of the village beneath the hill,
a return to a bygone age
where all we imagined remained there still.

It was a pilgrimage
even if we struggled in the car
and travelling wasted too much of the day.
"That's just the way things are"
you said. We were about halfway
stopping for lunch at noon
already resigned to our returning far too soon.

In the Hospice

Head bowed I withdraw, sadly
drained of the remnants of joy
harvested from recalling days gladly
spent with you. Now the smallest thing annoys;
the slightest sound
- each a rude assault upon your ear -
does nothing but confound.

Confused past patience, how can you bear
the discordant clatter of another
cup and saucer, the pleas of those ordering
capsules of relief? I remember a mother
and the way she would spontaneously sing,
happiest then with an audience of one
now only content with an audience of none.

In Mourning

There used to be a sparkle in your eye
fired by a vigorous joust with life.
And then I watched it die,
an unwilling witness as you lost your wife,
you so desperate to weep
inexplicably dry-eyed at being left behind.

She would have told you what to do: keep
looking to the future, your mind
alive, remorselessly focussed on how to spend
your time - and not waste it
as she feared she had in the end.

You say I cannot understand it,
how heavily it sits,
not death itself but the emptiness it commits.

On Being Asked To Prove Love

This fog, dense as any
in living memory, spawns improvident
thoughts. How many
others are left searching for the once self-evident?

Opaque enough to disguise hate
this ghostly world conspires
to heighten the primacy of fate
and sharpens my desire
to understand the workings of a mind
occluded by the harsher metrics of love.

Do I force you to be unkind
and demand newly conjured metaphors to prove
all those things you mean to me?
If so, should I exclude all those no longer there to see?

Unrequited Love

You offered nothing to suggest how love might grow.
Love - you said - *is a thin charade exposed by sudden leaving.*

Facing rejection, what could you bestow
on me to subdue this grieving
or see my paltry self-worth increase?
As dawn begins each day's gradual decay
what can halt my ragged fall as I cease
to hope and hope to fade away?

Raking through the relics in past emotions' store
I recall how feelings curdle and perish
and then I know, when there is nothing more
than landfill left for worms to cherish,
the only choice is for me to live out this lie
and wait for traitorous and unrequited love to die.

Defenceless Against Time

I never found the time
to comprehend the passage of night,
to decode the leasing of my life's prime
for the ever-greying white
of certainty. The duplicity of thieves
leaves time whimpering, unheard
above the rustle of fallen leaves,
a muted slipping from the stage without a word.
Cheap wisdom protests nothing can make
amends to arrest my going.

If there were practicalities to take
from this, their wisdom might see me growing,
able to make a more resolute defence
against my leaking time with so little recompense.

Orienteering

The map offers no clues to where we are.
You'd said "let's get out and live!"
your zeal robbing me of time to prepare,
to challenge the equation which balances give
and take, recognition that Life is on a lease.
You point to where we lately were,
a finger tracing our ambitions's vague decrease
as if what's left's a hardship we can bear.

There's no decay
in your smile, its mission to uphold
my spirits, to champion these days
grown sullen as they give way to cold.
How can I chart all that you know,
decipher the complex key that maps you so?

On Not Accepting Your Faith In The Stars

I was never struck
by your love of astronomy,
frustrated you'd not accept blind luck
steered our lives, that there's no heavenly quality
in the astrologists' tell.

Why not find meaning in the wind
or throw coins into a well?
Why not hope to find
a crystal ball in which to mystically derive
the magic of creative art?

Yours is not the forecast by which I intend to thrive.
I will never be a convert
to those stars by which you navigate
and to which you desire to make me subjugate.

Fearing Dementia

When it grows
it does so in each moment.
Disinterested in elaborate shows,
its practiced mantra is *no comment*.
Expanding, you might measure its increase
as easily as describe the sky.

I suffer the slurry of a slow decrease,
the shrivelling of memory,
yet plead with it to stay
as if it might be held by line of sight.

Some say there's wisdom in decay.

Unable to decipher another empty night
the morning finds me mesmerised again by you
and scared - one day - I'll find myself become someone new.

The Claims You Made

Strange how I never found a way
to make the most of our time
together. Subject to gradual decay,
that withering half-life bereft of rhyme
was filled with wasted hours
searching out a perfect sunset.

When I sent you flowers
you claimed them counterfeit,
said you could divine a petal's clumsy repair
coloured with impermanent marker pen.

When I said that you were fair
you claimed this as the forever lie of men
who lacked the passion, wit and skill
to understand love - and understanding, then fulfil.

Conversation With My Muse

When you come
is it to rescue me from the desert
of ideas or to remind me of the tomb,
encourage reassembling parts
of history behind myopic eyes?

Inadequate graces
weakly dovetail semi-blatant lies
from reimagined faces
made bankrupt by the trickster Age,
then fail to infuse this tongue
with anything more than clichéd love or rage.

I aspire to be freed by song
as if there might be words to slow down time,
and slowed, for retarded time to then be stopped by rhyme.

Frost & Fog

Surprised by the renegade day
you had expected a temperate
embrace, something more fitting for late May.
This chill has the air of a failed first date.

In the gathering grey nothing shines,
your hopes dimmed
as the sundial's vague shadow slowly declines.

Like a boat with sails untrimmed
you wallow and fade
becalmed in an all-consuming mist
leaving no trace but the shade
and shape of one hoping to be kissed.

Robbed of straight-edged horizon, what's left to see
but your blank life, still and frosted and solitary?

Constructive Criticism

Against a scratching post the big cat paws
sharpening its claws ready to protect its brood;
about its savage jaws
dried traces of incriminating blood.

In the back room the Writing Group meets
to discuss their relationship with time,
custodians picking at each other's work as if sour sweets
or doing so was a newly tolerated crime.

Later, the furrowing of your brow
accompanies the instinct to again take up a pen,
indulge the compulsion of an addict to allow
your whelp to be sacrificed to other less worthy men.

Why is there something that's always wrong,
your work's dissection leaving you impotent and unsung?

Compulsion

Abstracted from reality, he painted,
consumed by a passion
with which he had become compulsively acquainted.
A slave to fashion
he blamed heaviness of touch for rolling
inadequately with the punches,
failing to bob and weave and avoid their controlling
and non-instinctive hunches.

It's not important what's created
he claimed, in part confessing
an expectation to be defeated.
*In the end there is nothing
I can do to deny this shallow pleasure,
made slave to things I doubt anyone will treasure.*

The Shakespearian Lead

Backstage he summons his muse
silently mouthing the verse
he soon will use
to enslave us. His method - to rehearse
and then deliver - has no compare;
his interpretation of Elizabethan gems
a subtle talent all too rare.

Yet this borrowed stratagem
leaves him tortured by an urge to write
constantly unsure how fair
it is (enter stage right
spot-lit in the charged air
he fuels so well)
that *their* double-act is a billing guaranteed to sell.

New Moon, Old Anguish

The day dawns grey and already old
up to its usual tricks in ticking on the date.

Should there not be something to behold,
welcome evidence to extricate
me from this untimely purgatory?

A new month does little to calm a heart
whose irregular drumbeat taunts me.

Distracted by the excuse of Art
I keep busy, remain wary,
cursed by fragility beyond will,
subject to unmanufactured pedantry.

If I were not ill
I might boast of tyrant projects slain
and not fear the coming of the next new moon again.

Moving On

I wonder at what stage
you decided we should part;

was love undermined by rage
or the victim of a weary heart?

How can I say
or untangle wrong from right?

How can I know if such decay
was wrought from boredom's might?

Where is the need for eloquence
within a beating breast

if there's no recompense
against doubt honestly expressed?

Perhaps I should have been the first to quit
already undone by the supremacy of your wit.

Slam, Vulnerable

The trick is to meld
against a plaintive heart -
though what chance when the dearth of trump cards held
is testament to a dealer's art,
your slick-fingered skill
in skimming lies
from the bottom of the pack. *Still*
you say, diamonds in your eyes,
this hand is not yet done;
why should you not finesse me?

Ask me to eclipse the sun
or make spades from filigree;
both courses would be easier to chart
than vanquishing the Queen of Hearts.

Undercover Writer

Almost by subterfuge he starts.

Something other than modesty prohibits the kind of boast
popular in downtown bars,
improbable claims made by those most
likely to be ruined by rumours' spread.

Fumbling words through the needle's eye
he's compromised by their fraying thread;
spinning the loaded lexical die
he finds invisible bias might
see his most earnest wishes foiled.

Would just one triumph be quite
enough for the hours toiled,
the puzzles which remain unsolved,
the truths from which he's still one-step removed?

Falling Apart

Susceptible to the vagaries of yarn
I watch stitches slip from the loose knit
of affection, bear witness as its pattern
ladders with the haemorrhaging of wit.

All the while I hoped mine
would be the skill to save it,
deployed at the faintest sign
of intimacy slipping from the skein of the infinite.
In the warp and weft's moving
is mimicry of some kaleidoscopic aspect.

Unravelled, I follow the thread of our loving;
a purposeless trail with no respect
for how you once, so perfectly,
completed the weave of me.

Perspective

Listlessly I struggle from my bed
enslaved to being tired.

Yesterday there was a rupture in my head
as all hope simultaneously expired
and I was left to abide
in an uneasy truce with memory.

If my bloodshot eyes were open wide
the whole world is what I'd wish to see,
history in plain sight
- and in that haunting panoramic view
I'd seek the love I lost last night.

Were you still here, you'd emphasise this day was new
- then warn me not to tax my mind
in forlorn searching for past things I'll never find.

Heading into Winter

Wrestling with an unnamed plight
does nothing but disturb my rest.
Sunset finds me fearing night,
the agony of spending hours oppressed
and trying to escape the reign
of monsters lately subjugating me.

I should not complain
nor beg for mercy;
each morning still dawns bright,
crowned by the sun's trespass from heaven
to usurp malevolent night.
Yet still I stumble along this uneven
path, one which seems only to get longer
as I get weaker and not stronger.

Camelot's Phoenix

You paint mascara around your eyes
to camouflage your distraught state,
have music played loud to drown out your cries.
You choose not to curse the fate
that mutilated hope.

Where you once possessed
mythic and unconstrained scope
for wisdom, now you struggle to comprehend the least
of things and fail to vanquish others' shallow despising.

From this inauspicious state
I see you rising
to knock again at the castle gate,
be admitted for the harmony you yet might bring,
reclaim your rightful place at the table of the king.

Reparations

An idle thought
resurrected from a fragile past
is the long wished for guest who sought
to cauterise loyalty's waste
and staunch the flow
of might-have-beens. Through the porous night
you are tortured by sufficient woe
to dominate your sight,
the price you've paid writ large like the interest on a loan
with the principal lost for sure.

In penury you bemoan
the wealth you had before,
and hope to reinstate me as your friend
just as I was before our friendship's end.

Heart-to-heart

Others like to boast of broken hearts
as if trophies, their own now dead
and fractured into a multiplicity of parts
cast aside and buried.

They cultivate an artificial tear
conjured from a misty eye,
the outcome - it would appear -
of the mortal wound from a fatal lie.

My stubborn heart, kept artificially alive,
still misses beats now you are gone,
its sole remaining task to give
voice to being irretrievably alone.

Yet what of this does your heart see
immunised against the plague of my agony?

In Which She Mocks His Romanticism

The savage inclemency of the day
forces him to run for cover,
seek shelter from which to re-survey
the treacherous terrain of love and lover.

There was a time
when you'd take up your pen
and in unmetered rhyme
attempt to show you were the best of men...

What must I have thought
(the naivety of my age!)
to think she could be bought
by such ham-fisted equipage?
It takes more than words to prove
the breadth and depth and quality of love.

Comeuppance: Reality TV

Was it wise to be so unreservedly seen
stripped naked for every prying eye
- those addicted to jealousy's green -
while plundering contemporary alchemy
to mix dubious compounds for the ride?

Later, a sudden loss of face
was ruthlessly distilled into a need to hide;
being out-manoeuvred and in disgrace
I could only dismiss an inclination to perpetually shine.

If the mirror reveals a deepened brow
those easy-earned scars are mine.
It's an apt reflection which now
exposes popularity's cruel disdain
and proves humiliation's an indelible stain.

Eulogy for a Villain

The independence of the day
is untroubled by your pine-wood cloak
and the subtly meandering way
the crematorium's smoke
pencils to the sky. Unable to break
with tradition I stand to face
the congregation, am expected to speak
not of cheating or disgrace
but rather the nobility of grief.

How many of the black-clad feel your loss?
How many the selfishness in relief?
How many glance toward the cross
and proper in their mourning weeds
only feign forgiveness for your past deeds?

Mirror-talk

The damage is done.
Potential, dragged through the mud,
wears a dull overcoat, masking reflections from the sun.

You'd anticipated flowering from a bud
rather than this
wizening; imagined a reward allowing you to compare
expectation against life, the prize of knowing what's amiss.

Perhaps you wish your senses were
somehow without sense
while I - an inconsequential advocate -
remain unclear how you'll recommence
a journey you've come to hate.

Perhaps it's easier for you to let things be
and leave all the untangling to me.

Judgement Day (aged 16, 18, 21...)

If there was something to be gained
in being the final one,
the last envelope to remain;
if there was sufficient reward in opening it alone
to confront diminishing self-respect
or face down self-spite
or recognise the negative effect
of embracing un-timetabled delights;
if there was a prize in finally feeling free
I'd strive to camouflage the public shame
at this climax attached to me
- or apply to change my name
or seek a dodge of some unqualified sort -
and burn the damning end-of-term report.

Me, v9.0

Haunted by the simple delight
of unencumbered youth
I seek out its fragile ghost despite
knowing to search for its illusive truth
will consume my failing wit.
Chained by loss, what more
can I other than sit
and interrogate memory's store
for things once loved and things despised?
What can I give
to find myself unmesmerised
by the vapour of how I used to live?

Now there's nothing left to be
other than the latest iteration of me.

Première

Who would not aspire to invent
a radical new symphony of verse
lauded as truly excellent?
Queues would form to watch my choir rehearse
guided in pace and pause by me,
a conductor at the height
of his linguistic puppetry.
Romantic in the spotlight
such performances would enhance my worth,
reward me for the skill to innovate
and rise above the dearth
of brilliance I have produced to-date.
Yet persistent silence lengthens out my days
elongated by the absence of your praise.

Castaway

I have heard you sing
sea-shanties, though not to me.
I have seen you bring
togetherness, yet willingly
condemn me to live
in a vacuum of one.

What bounty can I give
you, shipwrecked and alone?
What can I hope to prove
and thus be freed to leave
this desolate outcrop of love?

I can deceive
only myself, sing this tuneless refrain,
and broken and washed-up therefore remain.

The Inevitable Covid Poem

How can it touch us all
this enemy we've never seen before?
How can some ignore the call
to prevent its spread? There is always more
that can be done
yet each new red line seems hesitantly drawn.
We listen to soundbites and, trapped at home,
fixate on graphs and charts, watch fears born
out, enacted by a ghostly thief
who turns wealth to poverty
and every day to grief.

Such assault may leave no evidence of injury,
but all-pervasive, indiscriminate, the data shows
it hunts us down, this most feared of foes.

The Would-be Poet (as a young man)

His hand trembles when he commits
words to the page. Hand on heart
he hopes his poetry befits
the rigours of an art
where victory is tortuously won.
Perpetually assailed
by doubts, he knows reason
can never be prevailed
upon to forbear
the rescuing of his befuddled youth
and the magic to be discovered there.
Camouflaged in myth, words guard truth
in inviolable secrecy:
Not all can know what it is to write and to be free.

Eulogy

It was her first experience of grief
and the departure of one so dearly
loved. Mourner-in-chief
at the cemetery, she had so nearly
held it together, resolved not to let others see
her distress. *I already miss her;
she meant so much to me.
And when I think of her
I know the best of the bargain
was mine. Any wonder then to be devastated by my loss?
You may laugh at me, treat with distain
this excess of fuss over an arthritic border-collie-cross,
but in the million she was the one
and now her death has left me all alone.*

Looking Back from Catbells

From the crest of the fell you can see
down to the lake where those unaffected
by the rugged hills' majesty
merely stroll, their eyes rarely directed
upward into the bright
and glorious show
of diamond-clear daylight,
to where glacier-faceted rocks glow
as if for this purpose alone they were made:
to honour the brilliance of the day.

Remembrance cowers in the lake-side shade.
Thwarted still, it's here I choose to stay
recalling how on the hills I once felt free
your hand in mine the greatest of symphonies.

When he chose not to go

Who would have thought
his reluctance to move away
from here would have wrought
in her such firm resolution not to stay?
Her decision become a final stand
reminded him of miserable infancy,
an only-child homeland
resurrected as mirror of a life so solitary.

Why he had not thought
his choice would see her gone?

Bereft, his anguish wrought
new tunes from desolation's moan,
orchestrated anthems in the slow
and unyielding tempo of loneliness and woe.

Weather Report

My back was turned when you doused the fire.
Knowing I could not abide
the cold, you ignored my plea, the desire
for heat, amused to observe my slide
into despair. The embers' glow long gone
you find me searching fruitlessly
for sparks of life, pacing attic rooms alone
in a blizzard of melancholy.

If, in dreaming, combustion reoccurred
to melt the frozen wastes of my insanity,
soon enough reality took hold, and though assured
a glimmer of the old me
somewhere yet remained, there were no reasons to be glad
as love's hearth was still impossibly cold and sad.

Battle of the Sexes

We spoke of the righteousness of war.
Neither out of mind nor out of sight
we languished at the hotel bar
each shot boosting convictions we were right
the others' argument a blatant lie,
truth corrupted by part-occluded eyes.

How could you deny
my reasoning when yours - propaganda and lies
so coldly delivered -
ignored the primacy of the heart?
How could you be so determined
that we should part
and - in playing your part
to perfection - contrive to break my heart?

Between the Pear and the Cheese

It was about time I took
control over the 'this', the 'that', and the 'other';
reasons for not declaring myself. Look,
I had no ambition to smother
you with some corny romantic feast
the hero dish the skewering of my heart.
All I wanted was for you, my guest,
to play your part
and savour a meal crafted from the recipe for love.

Was it fear or naïvety that compelled me
to await the pause before the cheese to make my move,
that unmenu'd delicacy
which you chose to slight
still sated on the taste of pear Angel Delight.

Brain-washing

How far did they go out of their way
to pursue me? How persuasive was their devotion's thrust?
Sufficient for me to stay
with them, abandon my life to their trust.

Later, harsh lessons: discovering vapid rituals are
natural precursors to grief;
that naïvety and being unaware
are opportunities for thieves
to corrupt conviction's treasure chest.
Each stolen tenet was hardly priceless art,
yet such relics once warmed my breast.

The absence of those self-defining parts
succumbed to paralysis, a compound fear
of losing everything once held dear.

Love's impossible equation

How did it come
to this, a myriad of small defects
compounded to an inaccurate sum
which in all emotional respects
even a mathematician could only parse
as flawed? In my mind's eye
this unsolvable equation is
hardly complex (unlike Gravity's
laws or Moments' reign) yet here,
still working in the margins, my heart
is unsettled by an instinctive fear
that ineptitude will again play its part.

Being unable to prove the logic of Love's natural laws
is hardly a rallying cry to my cause.

Mourning those things I didn't know I'd miss

Do you only see you've lost your way
when you reach an 'end'?
If found moping and alone, what would you say
to reassure a friend
you'd not been swamped by woe?

Forgive me
if I tell less than I know
about my solitude, shamed by the indignity
of having so little concrete on
which to now rely. Although needing to hide
from you each and every groan
(and still not knowing what keeps you from my side)
be sure you'll never quit my unsettled mind
nor will the myriad of other things I've left behind.

The Hare become the Tortoise

You'd ignore the democratic offence
and - being addicted to unruly speed -
cast off compliance
and relegate common sense below your need
to constantly find
a permanent antidote to going slow.

More than a zephyr, you'd wind
along the country roads you know
too well - until that day when reckless pace
skittled you from a bend. Who made
you abandon the race
and broken, ride side-saddle on a piebald jade?
Better to go slow
they said, *than to never go.*

"The Magpie"

You are offhand about the tarnished key
which opens the padlock to your treasure,
and with practiced distain survey
others' chattels seemingly devoid of pleasure
apparently unmoved by the rare
the bejewelled, the platinum-set.

Yet all the while you are
dissembling, slave to that glinting carcanet
which ornaments your iron-bound chest
the strongbox in which you hide
your beloved and blessed,
manifestations in carats of hallmarked pride.

Unbridled, your avarice's limitless scope
finds you always scavenging with lustful hope.

A Kind of Dorian Grey

How were you made?
Rumour has it you tend
to prefer shadow and shade
as if light might lend
itself to expose some surface counterfeit
and compromise you.

Would such enlightenment reset
an internal (or infernal!) clock anew
and return you to some inaugural year
corrupt the current variation of yourself on show?

If you chose self-preservation, to disappear,
there would be much you'd never know
including my own ineffectual part
in trying to thaw your frozen and un-ageing heart.

Ageing Ungracefully

Why does it always seem
time ought to have more to give
as if we're owed tokens to then redeem
against special offers on how we live?

The softest pastel dye
dusts the frail petals of roses
with kisses bestowed wantonly
- just as preconceptions of beauty discloses
tropes on form and style and show.

Subject to merciless tides, colour fades
ungraciously from both the rose and our prime, and so
exposes how fragile we are made.
Corrupted by unremitting longing for our youth
we beg more time, try vapours bought at the expense of truth.

Heritage

You stroll around monuments
plugged into a podcast of history's rhyme
enchanted by the contents
of cabinets that strive to usurp time.
Labels promote impossible dates as if to overturn
erosion of silver, fabric, masonry
- as if such simple time-travel could burn
the scars of the past onto your memory.

Legends of love, politics, or enmity
are soaked into the walls of every room;
emotions carbon-dated for posterity
occasionally triumph over the doom
of years, allowing them to rise
and - for just a moment - replay themselves before your eyes.

A Casanova's Main Course

Before the inevitable side-effects, the quack said
the first thing to go would be my appetite.
Initially, generous portions allayed
my fears, allowed me to think I might
order double rations, click my fingers for the bill
as if unconcerned about cost, revelling in the fullness
of my heart. Over-indulgence was a way to kill
time, to avoid being trapped in the dullness
of repetition - and in wondering how broken I'd eventually be.
Embracing the challenge to seek out the new
I truffled for the unusual, the unexpected. To see
deep into the promise of others I came to view
their menus voraciously, asking Love's chef to take special care
in preparing my entrée not medium but rare.

Dante's Muse Speaks

His grotesque pen-portraits tend
to show victims prone, consumed by desire,
bound by the hypnotic, compelled to spend
their days in torture, required
to subjugate themselves to the witching-hour.

Why should it be different for you?

You protest innocence with a sour
face, attempt ingratiation with a fond adieu.
Did you harbour the misguided thought
my rules might not apply? Did you suppose
- against all the evidence - aught
could be done in the face of my supremacy? Speak to those
who have tried to fight my will
and you will find them broken, lost, and weeping still.

Stockholm Syndrome

If you turned me to a slave
trapped within your web of pleasure
what would I say? If what you craved
- as the epitome of leisure -
was to have me at your beck
and call, I'd gladly sacrifice my liberty.

Although currently compelled to check
you've done yourself no injury,
that you're well-fed and strong,
perhaps at some future time
you too will confess you belong
here, that my dedication supersedes my crime,
and your life - far from being a living hell -
is testament to love expressed so well.

Snapshot in the Institution's Garden

The unspoken question is
whether the viewer is sufficiently beguiled
or is forced to remark that something seems amiss,
teased by sepia hints of the child
you may have been. And there too; look.
Beyond the trees, the low sun,
the sudden reflection from the cover of a book
you have just put down, as if you were done
and finished, wanting to say
something about the story, to put it in a frame
and carry it away. They
tell me you are often the same
when revelling in such rare and lucid days
searching for a memory from which to earn their praise.

On the Isthmus

There is romance in standing on the shore
wrapped against the chill from the end
of a solitary day, those moments before
having to contend
with rapidly fading light
the distant hills crowned
by a setting sun. When I gave up the fight
I accepted life would confound
the florid expectations of my youth,
its failures etched upon my brow
each deep line a scar of unvarnished truth.

Did your sudden departure mow
down remnants of fragile hope, leave me to stand
alone and grim and cold - and longing for your hand?

Insomnia

You left the bedroom window open
permission for the night
to enter, to soothe broken
dreams, repair memory's line-of-sight.

Such a trick will never work for me.

Only defeating the compulsion to pry
into your secret history can cure me
of this cancerous nocturnal jealousy.
If sleep remains my great
ambition, finding myself awake
is ignominious defeat.

This is torture I cannot brake.

You hid slumber's keys elsewhere
ensuring lasting peace for me is never near.

Lonely Hearts Ad

If you allowed your eyes
to scan the paper and find the part
where ads boast foolproof remedies
for a shattered heart
would you think of mine?
How often you held it to account
or asked me to define
what it meant to love! I could never surmount
your challenges. Indeed
wouldn't all the heroes of antiquity
(about whom you've never read)
be overwhelmed by such iniquity,
choose to look elsewhere for a thread of praise
and the promise of more enlightened days?

Gawain's Farewell

One year on, it's time for armour now,
for unbreakable vows to be re-sworn.
If there is upon my brow
not the brightness of the morn
it has been usurped by the residue of night
and dream's dark shadows. My King,
it may be trial beyond your sight
yet honour-bound I'll ride through burgeoning Spring
certain of duty. Is there a need to fortify
resolve or hone my knife -
or rather wipe from memory
remembrance of this blessed life?
Already I have forgotten all I've ever seen
subsumed by ominous thoughts of the knight of green.

"Baz Woz 'Ere"

You see this Dutch Bond defaced
and bemoan an Age
permitting perfect patterns to be razed
in the flourish of anonymous aerosol rage.
Where is the gain
to be had in flirting with the whore
of vandalism? Is such expression the new main-
stream, or - limited or limitless - a store
of part-baked words the product of a state
which stumbles toward decay
in post-Pop Art screaming? Should we ruminate
on meaning and see these images as a way
to protest freedom or entrapment? You choose:
heads they win and tails you lose.

Elizabethan

Staring out across the churning sea
you conjure an image of vast naval power.
To realise that dream you issue a heart-felt plea
selling your vision to the flower
of our youth, knowing you'll send many out
to spend their final days
in selfless and stout
defence of the realm. But then, fearing loyalty's decay
in the face of brutal attack,
you imagine some scared young men like castaways hid.

If there is no going back
from here, let nothing forbid
our Triumph, memories burnished by glorious might
in days when Victory heralded a future bright.

Remembering Authenticity

We cry
when we are born
and soon enough find jollity
easily forsworn,
led astray by misplaced
faith and the lure of vainglorious and trumpeted
ambition. Are we disgraced
when accepting honesty disabled
by plastic prophets of authority,
the seduction of unattainable skill?
Why is simplicity
in adulthood regarded as an ill?
When all the tinselled trappings are gone
are we not the best of ourselves alone?

Mining for Truth

And if I choose to live
beyond the seductions of impiety,
to free the shackles, achieve
contentment in this fragile crystalline society
of ours, must I also turn the other cheek,
embrace a less-than-rosy hue,
tolerate those who seek
shallow masquerades to willingly accept as true?

The only defence I have is
the blood running through my veins.
My dreams, as fallible as yours or hers or his
direct my thoughts. Worthwhile gains
come from panning for gold, their comforts to be had
by filtering nuggets of good from bad.

An Optimist Falls Into March

The turning year's darkness outworn
by Spring, a watery light begins to now
recharge us with hope born
from pale colours borrowed from a sunrise brow,
the resurrection of the seeming-dead.

You talked of getting away,
conjured exotic images in your head
of sun and vibrance. All seemed gay
when sketched as picture-postcard scenes
to which you'd cling. But is your dream as true
as this resurgent green
teasing with its promise of the new,
toying with what may be in store -
a year so much better than all those years before!

On the Red Carpet

Pause, pose, smile; accentuate the view
you gift the cameras, a down-payment to mend
broken promises or give them what's due
(or expected) for choosing to commend
past performance. If later you are crowned
the award will be your own,
a triumph to confound
the doubting critics; you'll have shown
thespian dexterity and strength of mind
to excel at the fakery of celluloid deeds.

And if you lose will you be kind
to the victor, wrestle free from the weeds
of jealousy lurking beneath the satin of the show,
tell yourself each defeat is an opportunity to grow?

Tea and scones for two?

Perhaps sleeping in the afternoon's a defect;
perhaps my health's just middling-to-fair;
perhaps my friends suspect
there's falsehood in this self-confident air.
Do they disapprove
of my attempts to hold back time
and repair the chipped veneer of love
given I'm well beyond my prime?

Trapped in the purgatory of shortening days
and praying for my store of years to be re-charged,
I suffocate in a vacuum of their praise.

Is it so wrong to want esteem enlarged
and take up arms against a world that shows
the flaws and failures of one who can no longer grow?

And so I

How many have been woken in the dead
of nightmare by some dream-shattering yell?
How many felt alarmed? And so I fled.
How could I dwell
in a haunted house if it was not
the haven it once had been? And so
I threw old memories aside, forgot
the best of days, and from self-indulgent woe
scatter-shot in verse
clumsy images moulded from the clay
of insubstantial words. And so I rehearse
as if rehearsal postpones decay,
permission granted to bemoan
what little there is here now that you have gone.

No way back

No matter if I recite
phrases from Cupid's playbook of love,
none will save me now. Once quite
easy for me to side-step truth and prove
fidelity, now seeing all I said had been a lie
you've banished me to a blistering desert
of arid truth. If I
could use my wit to impart
a fresh - yet tragic - backdrop to this
my story, would you still know it was untrue
as if dishonesty is all there's
left when it comes to my relationship with you?

Such fissures might see me sally forth
and ask - were I so inclined - what it is love's really worth.

The Song of the Poet in Political Exile - I

My ambition had been to travel and behold
the Extraordinary - then have people hang
on my retelling: wrapt, oblivious to cold
or damp or heat as I sang
of truth throughout the day.
But then north, south, east and west
merely offered routes to get away,
to escape the ignorance of those who rest
seemingly content - yet suffer in the fire
and brimstone of others' sharp lies.

Is it fair that they expire
while I, by and by,
strive to grow increasingly strong
cocooned in a selfish life backing-tracked by song?

The Song of the Poet in Political Exile - II

On pause under house arrest
I recall how it felt to break away,
doors unlocked by keys of self-interest.
Facing more confinement, I stay
where I must and suffer incessant review
of unrelenting criticality,
a punishment I judge unfairly due.

How might such discomfort sit with me
were I to calculate the balance of my life?
If I was dead,
cut from living by the sharpest knife,
how would I be remembered?

If all I leave behind are words, I hope each phrase contains
a glimpse of truth sifted from the ashes of my remains.

On White Scar

Sometimes you feel betrayed when life
shifts its ground
removes us from certainty, injects intangible strife;
crude punishment for a wayward patient found
far from the ward, blissfully happy, searching for home!

Knowing somewhere there is treasure
what if I choose to search for it alone
along the way mistake solitude for pleasure
or miss prizes hidden in plain sight?

Occasionally we stop to look
surprised by unforeseen delight,
forget the stumbling steps we took
to get here. I will always recall that White Scar day
and the view which stole my breath away.

Blah, blah, blah

Does obstructive pride
prevent meaningful change,
whitewash opinion? If you choose to brush aside
my theorems that is not strange
given our views no longer remain the same.

Before, ensnared in linguistic bindweed
I missed opportunities to clear my name,
chose false logic to proceed
as I always had with you.

But now there is surely merit in my argument,
pushing back against your new
and unwholesome reality. Ha! You still think I spent
my time living by a philosophy grown old
and never listening to what I was being told.

Subject Matter: Memoir

How well you wear
the disappointment from the years you waste!
When will it become too hard to bear
this empty grind? You don't conceal a distaste
for the flimflam show
yet plunder the landfill of memory
to reconstitute the scenes you've known.

And now you have decided there is falsehood in eternity.

What of the ability to retain
those precious shards you find
fused within scrapyard of the brain?
What of the mavericks lurking in the deep recesses of your mind?

If you took the trouble to look
you might preserve them all between the covers of a book.

Pickpocket of Plagiarism

In shabby disguise you stalk the muse
hoping to steal from others' verse

and, deconstructing, use
them as your own. But contraband words disperse

and leave you mute, your inability to sing
echoes a bird who cannot fly

harnessed to a broken wing
yet with memories of soaring majesty.

Frantically you compile
line upon line of poetic mimicry

drugged by rhythm, seduced by style
and how you think your words should be.

You chunter on, fail to advance
imagining progress in blissful ignorance.

Dancing to the Tune

There is redundancy in literary first-aid
impotence in advice's grace
when wasted on themes decayed
unable to find a place
of sanctuary. Thus nothing in your argument
can prevent me from taking up this pen
and - compelled to invent
another self - plunge again
into that realm where a single word
can, like a faller's parachute, give
salvation. You say I cannot afford
to live as I would choose to live;
but there is nothing I can do, I say,
shackled as I am, and always in the Piper's pay.

A Farewell Letter

I needed to be distanced to write
to you, at the letter's foot scrawl my name
- as if you might
not know who it was from! Recognition is not fame
of course, but infamy; and treason is
the weightiest cross I have to bear.

Yet I do not wish this
letter (my paltry emissary) to appear
as proxy pleading. Just know you kept me afloat
when I was taken by the tide;
your caring, my lifeboat.

Island-bound on the shipwreck of my pride
I am resolved to fade away
hoping my treachery will - like me - gradually decay.

Recipe

It was as if I had resolved to make
a cake but found the eggs were rotten.
I rescued what I could. Yet how could I take
comfort in that, knowing I'd forgotten
to source all ingredients needed? "You have
an unhealthy ambition," you said, "which when you die
you'll take unfulfilled to your grave
having lived nothing but a half-baked lie."

Is there no merit in my part-blended verse?
Nothing tempting you to read
no matter how much mixing I might rehearse?
Not only is my output seemingly insipid,
the ink has dried and crusted in my pen -
spur enough to see you enraptured by other men.

Pen-portraits

You liked to think you'd been blessed by a muse
who would over-look
your work, ensure you'd use
their wisdom to craft a book
of which to be proud. Yet there was no golden hue,
no critics queuing at your door to praise
what you had done. Looking anew
at how you'd spent your writing days,
the way your characters had been devised
from folk you knew, I offered to lend
a second voice to help, sympathised
with your striving to make the muse your friend.

In the end we found we'd both been used
and you by fickle fate disgracefully abused.

Balance Sheet

It was short-term cash you said you'd need
to meet tough exponential targets set,
to face down pressure to exceed
all expectations. You measured debt
in a photoshopped report,
called spending 'investment' to show
not a falling short
but a foolproof plan to grow.

It was a shallow canvas allowing you to impute
traditional methods and strike your critics dumb.

Did you assume if made mute
they would take their chatter to the tomb,
play the naïve victims of your pecuniary lies
and ignore all the shady dealings you'd devised?

The Magician's Would-be Biographers

They were always expecting more
from you
and the breath-taking store
of tricks from which your reputation grew.

They longed for you to dwell
on the jail-broken myths behind your glory,
begged you to tell
them all the secrets of your rabbit-hatted story.

Thwarted and jealous, they chose to rewrite
your history and make it clear
where McGuffins were hid; assumed the wit
to try your tricks, yet spilled cards everywhere.

Their failure teetered between blessing and curse,
a loss of credibility for better or for worse.

"you leave something of yourself in the marks you make"

Unfolding the paper, the world fell still
mesmerised by eloquently compiled
marks where your pen - light as a quill -
had etched softly, rhythmically. To be filed
as keepsake, I wrapped your words
in tissue, aiming to one day bask again
in the glow such treasure should afford.

Yet now I wonder how you beguiled your pen
to dance so lightly on the tightrope of true
and false, of less and more.
I thought I had known you
but that was in my life before
you unleashed your ink, when respect
was not vulnerable to a smudge of cause and effect.

Mining Memory

Excavation came via blank verse,
took possession and threw you
back into a dream. It was the reverse
of memory, deepening as it grew,
conundrums unresolved by your attempts to write.

Did you wish your words would rouse the dead,
free skeletons closeted in the night,
leave you astonished
at the conjured ghost
who jousted with your intelligence?
Would it be too much to boast
that reliving the past was recompense
for anguish buried in each lode-bearing line,
the perils of excavation in such a treacherous mine?

Ambition Misaligned

You dreamed of possessing
a magic key with which to estimate
the future, to permit releasing
of ambiguous bonds of indeterminate
measure. You yearned for the granting
of wishes though deserving
no reward, habitually wanting
it all, constantly swerving
the truth, expecting everything yet knowing
nothing; ignorance, mistaking
motivation for progress. Growing
desperate only leads to the making
of stories designed to flatter -
and ultimately confusing what does and does not matter.

Lancelot, on leaving Camelot

Who is not deflated by subdued light,
wounded by loose tongues' scorn,
left longing for a noble fight
or perilous crusades where the self can be forsworn?

In childhood, acquainted
with the Happy Ending's story,
we fail to recognise fables are tainted
with the eggshell veneer of glory.

Vaulting ambition leaves us too
blind to decipher the world as clearly
as we might. And so with nothing left to do
but execute the banishment of me,
usurped from the place where I belong,
I pay the price of corrupting right with wrong.

Methods of Self-Defence

There is comfort in finding fault,
pointing out offence
in others to halt
self-examination, critique become defence
against exposing poorly camouflaged ills.
You relish avoiding challenge and change,
believe your better self will
remain intact; permit strange
incantations to slip from your tongue,
observations designed to dwell
just on the righteous side of wrong.
Who can foretell
the price you pay for avoiding internal debate,
the sifting of self-love from the perils of self-hate?

After the Interview

You settle on the answer to their question now -
but all too late. Its omission leaves you cross.
And why you departed with that obsequious little bow
of gratitude still leaves you at a loss!
Anger vanquishes sorrow,
and in its battle with loose-virtued woe,
predicts bad news for tomorrow.

Appointment might allow you to overthrow
your current demons at long last,
a safety-valve for all the simmering spite
tainted just enough to sour the taste
of what you do now - and might
yet do next. In the end it rises, this uncompromising woe,
expecting failure - and believing it will always be so.

A Gambler's Faith

Having mistaken blind luck for skill
coincidence assailed you with sufficient force
to persuade that some instinctive will
would ensure henceforth you picked the winning horse;
that you'd realise a life full of pleasure
indulgence and rest,
future bank statements the perfect measure
to set you apart as the best
of punters. Superior to me,
you assumed fate would underwrite the cost
of wagering, thought investments would leave you free
to saunter and swagger, to boast
about what you'd buy, the holidays you'd take,
all funded by the money you'd inevitably make.

I did not see her leave

They castigated me for keeping away,
assumed those weasel words of mine
were just excuses fabricated to stay
distanced from the skeleton she'd become. It was a sign
of selfishness, they said, compounded by the wrong
of leaving open-ended at the end
past questions whose answers must belong
to the closure on which my future now depends.

Yet peace and closure for whose mind
when justification of a lie
is hard? What if you were to find
I simply could not accept that she would die
nor concede subservience to such an unnatural blot -
especially if ignoring it could keep her more secure than not?

History in a Packing-Case

Seldom is our history entirely true
if disguised to portray a fresher face.
Seduced by the new
I succumbed to the lure of a different place
where I could allow my eye
to see, revised in brick and stone, the change
I wanted engineering in my life's story.

Yet soon this new house will veer from strange,
normalised by title, deed and decree,
and so disqualify that plan for me to dwell
another somewhere where life might let me be.

One day biography's unravelling will tell
a different tale, one toward which I must grow
to hope to put the best of me on show.

On taking on an allotment

There is magic in usurping the none,
in adopting a neglected canvas to show
- stone by back-aching stone -
some modest transformation. The work is slow,
subject to weather's airs and graces,
to the constant riddling of expense,
of exertion, ruddied faces
as the spade digs for excellence
as it might for treasure. Triumphs are sweet,
short-lived, like rolling a loaded die
and hoping for a six. To meet
adversity with dignity
is aligned to repetitious deeds
and an incessant battle with remorseless weeds.

Politic's Greasy Pole, July 2022 - I

Was there once a boundary of shame
beyond which those who rose
to stellar heights dared not cross? Today a name
in lights requires elegant fonts to enclose
slippery meanings, and days
are spent treating honour as a non-contact sport,
chasing dodgy investments in buying praise
- or a straight-flush of A's in an end-of-term report.

The small print betrays honourable members got
no more than an 'F' in Integrity,
more persistent failure than temporary blot.
Witness their message-massaging, the hope none will see
that a road ploughed by privilege
gifts them so much more than a modest edge.

Politic's Greasy Pole, July 2022 - II

Treating truth with wantonness
is like playing lip-service to the rules of sport
choosing those which impact less,
compliance to all a matter of last resort.
Does a regular audience with the Queen
guarantee veneration of esteemed
colleagues? For friends to deny what they had seen?
To sacrifice all once deemed
inviolable? Is that the opiate which led you to betray
honesty the way you did, to translate
it to another tongue, deflect criticism away
and turn dishonesty to a Department of State?
If so, what would be the Minister's brief? Perhaps to sort
the chaff from the wheat in another redacted report.

Politic's Greasy Pole, July 2022 - III

"What a few months it's been"
says one. Another, "Make that a year!
Unlike anything I've ever seen,
all shit and no Shinola anywhere!"
Then the sage: "Just give it time;
as quickly as we saw the frenzy decrease
so the lure of becoming prime
mover will see vapid moral posturing increase."
"Will you stand?" asks one. "Me?!
I don't think so Old Fruit;
I've already played that game - and not so tunefully.
Better to keep my counsel and stay mute.
And if I'm forced to publicly cheer
I'd rather do so from afar than too near!"

The Green Man

March warmth is his cue to spring
from hiding as gardeners trim
and plant and tidy, and everything
verdant begins to burgeon around him.

There are narcotics in that smell!
Hallucination in kaleidoscopic viridian hues!

We unearth legends to tell
children how he grew,
how petals are his palette: the yellow and white
of daffodils, the journey through pinks to rose.
We submit ourselves to naïve delight,
imagine him dancing with those
who long to while their time away
with music, song, and play

The Coming of Winter

In desolation we chide
the wind. Decomposing flowers' smells
echo the corruption of Autumn's pride,
of heady scents which dwell
only in the mind or in those colours dyed
by paint on paper, the artist's hand
tracing with bristle and hog's hair
an imperfect monument to stand
weak against winter's inevitable despair.

Fragrance and beauty both
are stolen on the breath
of November winds, growth
an impossible promise. Death
is there for all to see,
the wonders of Spring merely memory.

Miners Greeting the Dawn

The shift impossibly long
self-discipline our only ally against nights
of black, the camaraderie of tired song
lifting us to daylight.
Again we ask if hard cash redeems
those bleak hours spent
underground; whether self-esteem
can be bribed with pecuniary argument.

There are rumours of another survey,
plans for another shaft there
beyond the engine shed; more decay
for the land, for us. And everywhere
we feel the fissures of life
as if we're gradually being dissected by a knife.

Sifting through the Sand

The flowers were intended to make amends
even if their colours had been dyed.
'Is that enough?' I asked. 'It depends'
you said, remaining dignified,
expecting I had more to say.
Experience told me things were seldom fixed
by words alone when truth lay
inevitably intermixed
with lies. Was it better to play dumb?

I imagine being addicted to archaeology,
excavating from the tomb
of our love relics that tell me not who to be
but offer sand-blown glimpses of how
I once navigated from then to now.

From the edge of the meadow

A gentle meadow-fold changes its seeming;
foreshortened, distances appear
- dishonest. Yet our esteeming
of its beauty remains undimmed. Everywhere
a delicate daub of spring
colours proffers benevolence, lays
our mind to rest, makes us want to sing
of the perfection of days.

A few brief hours from now
this vibrancy will fade, and night
emerge from beneath a field-edged bough
to temper our delight,
to overlay its shadow on our tongue,
force us to sing a more melancholy song.

Writer-in-residence

Ambition demands the setting forth
of credentials, badges worn with pride,
an independent measure of worth.
In the Reference Section you sit beside
volumes filled with fact and write
- fiction. Your avatar offers a brave face
when wrestling with characters not quite
emerging as imagined. Persuaded there's no disgrace
in creating skeletons to later mend,
dip further into the creative well.
Unruffled competence is the persona you tend
to favour, a passport permitting you to tell
others how it is - or in isolation sit
head-down, working, and making the most of it.

In an Italian Cathedral

She seems old beyond old
lying in state for damp-eyed
pilgrims who trek through unseasonal cold
their sleeve-worn belief soaked with pride.
Which of them asks exactly how she turned
from modest girl to being seen
as paragon, her image burned
upon this city's psyche? An unnatural shade of green
fogs the glass. Beyond, the frail skeletal hand
that one Sabbath was perceived
to move; a finger stand
erect and point to those who'd been deceived,
whose lack of faith and dread
was an insult to the dead.

Free Will

Is it perfect idolatry
to believe unvarnished logic can show
how all things should be?

You may choose to say so.

Though perhaps, if pressed, you'd be kind
enough to concede potential excellence
where reason's unconfined
by rule; accept a difference
of opinion; cease to object that an argument
constructed from mere words
yet leaves a residue once their force is spent.

There are no limits words afford
when experimenting with them alone,
manipulating physics in a universe of one.

Banquo's Ghost on The Witches

'tis time, 'tis time,
untie the winds and let them fight -
not merely soundbites from some Bardic rhyme
(a tale of castles, murder, knights)
this is menace at its best
in harrowed brow
and faltering voice expressed.

If only you'd not been caught in the 'now'
my friend, the blindness of prophecies;
nor swept along, future's prefiguring
blurred in the mist of your occluded eyes.

Hear them chant - *and now about the cauldron sing!* -
and prepare for the calamity of days
and the doom-laden perils of false praise.

Similarities between Politicians & Poets

They dreamed of immortality of the soul,
feasted on Halcyon days yet to come;
they sacrificed control
in their trek toward pastoral doom.
Yes, for a while their words endured
but they ignored the presage
of a darker future, remained sublimely self-assured.

Now comes another Age
playing fast-and-loose with time
as scribes and would-be scribes
wrestle against the primacy of rhyme.
With followers of their myopic tribes
they seek to build themselves a monument,
pay lip-service to all good words already spent.

Curtain Call?

To switch in and out of character
requires a resilient and energetic spirit.
Bated-breathed, we register
the shifts you make, recognise merit
in deceptions almost divine.

And then we try to do the same,
seek our slice of glory in some minor spotlight's shine.

Yet more than just a change of name
or reading scripts rescued from a battered case,
success demands embracing an alternate age
subsumed into another place.

Forced from the naked page
by scenes for which we were not bred
witness our ham-fisted mimicking render ambition dead.

From the trenches

Do we have the quarrelsome heart
for war? How will we later qualify
the decision to depart
our homes, fight for a lie
when the heavy guns are ranged
towards us and the shelling starts again?
Brutalities are exchanged,
principles soaked in the indelible stain
painted on us by those who reigned -
or those who wish to. Map tints are curated from blood
and dyed into uniforms stained
with patriotism. We recall the righteousness of good
yet remain unresolved that in answering its call
we have to be prepared to sacrifice it all.

Valentine

I remember when I first saw you there
sudden from the periphery come into view.
No-one had been dear
to me 'til then; now here was someone new
who might take my rustic truth
and artlessly refine it. Above
all else, this feeling transcends the folly of youth
suggesting something more than love -
perhaps the treasure from a rainbow's end
excavated from life's grind
by this new-found forever-friend.

Will I soon find myself unconfined,
at last free to be my best
when I lay my liberated heart upon your breast?

The Rechargeable Battery

Is it habit or fashion to chide
me for supposed misdeeds?
The unique way you provide
emotion's comfort also breeds
contempt, the motto of your brand.
In darkness I am subdued
by the back of your hand
as still I long for hope to be renewed
not shattered by that extra drink.
You claim mortal infection
leaves no chance to think
for yourself, nor settle on the correction
that might one day set you free

and let you see what has become of me.

"A Dummy's Guide to Imposter Syndrome"

I've had my fill
of Alchemists' promises to soothe my brow
and chase away these shadows of ill
feeling. Is there no potion to allow
me to live unconstrained, to strive
for and find the melody of a sweeter tongue?

How to make my creations feel alive?

How can all my work still seem wrong
when I have taken so much care,
when I have teased at words' most subtle sense
and stitched them into phrases that are
the ultimate I can dispense?
Will they eventually say I was not bred
for this, damnation only coming when I am dead?

Monsters in the Dark

Rarely out of mind
your malevolent spectre prowls about
and even were I blind
still I could seek you out
evidenced in my misstepping heart
insecure like a broken latch.

No matter we're apart
those treacherous vows we took still catch
me out, and always at the edge of sight
I fear the coming of a creature
who might yet haunt my night.

Does this echo need few features
to be a replicant of you,
a monster feeding once again on all that is untrue?

Viewers' Vote

You think she smiles just for you,
seducing with her screen-toned flattery
as if veneer is the epitome of true.
Out-of-shot, modern alchemy
readies potions for her to digest,
their mission to continually reassemble
her against the most recent template of 'the best'.

Fawning, you strive to assemble
yourself as her ghost, seeing
if you can sculpt make-up
or tone muscle to satisfy this mass-agreeing
fashion. Her prize is a loving cup,
and as the cameras pan away from sin
paid adverts message us: *let the games begin*.

The Toss of a Coin

Mischance weaves itself into a cheap lie
when truth proves the dearer.
Perhaps that's why
little is ever clearer
after misfortunes and accidents
indiscriminately waylay paupers and kings.
Randomness unravels the best of intents,
the most grand and most humble of things.

Gambling against luck's tyranny
is an uneven duel, yet I try my best
to joust with uncertainty,
stay in a game that's a one-sided contest
and hope by doing so
my chance of being fortunate will grow.

On Once Requited Love

Is it thanks to the subterfuge of minds
that the trump cards of love
are dealt from the bottom of the deck? That one finds
infatuation impossible to remove
like a broken-heart-shaped birthmark?

Submission leaves us shaken
like a dog without its bark
and silence for passivity is mistaken.

Betrayed by a blush of cheeks
alarms toll as stealthy calamity comes
to herald long and drawn-out weeks
on the path to self-inflicted soft-centred doom.
Is that when we finally discover nothing's proved
not even that once we loved?

At the Garden Gate

Weighing the importance of it all
provokes my decision to pay
an unexpected call,
to see if on this blustery day
my wager that our minds
and hearts are twinned will be settled right.
Yet there is something in these tuneless winds
blowing leaves in and out of sight
which drags expectation down.
Uncertainties accumulate
into the compound of a frown.
It is only hesitancy I hate
- that, and this impulse to prove
whether or not your doorbell heralds love.

Watching You Sleep

Both of us were keen
to bed - for you it was to satisfy an urge
circumstantially seen:
to purge
the tyranny of fatigue. There is sweetness
in the sight of your feeding
on sleep, usurping wakefulness,
while I, like an addict needing
my fix, anticipate
every breath. Reassured
by your calm recumbent state
I know soon you'll be cured
of today's misunderstandings - and that, restored to true,
I will again be able to enjoy the best of you.

Olympic Redemption

We were undone by your televised tears,
your loosing everything within.
Was defeat evidence of your fears
coming true, that you could not win
no matter how committed?
Convinced you'd never
tried harder, your country's colours fitted
like a skin, but neither they nor competition's fever
could magic your loss untrue.

Now four years on, you say you're better
than ever, talent born anew;
take your place at the start with greater
conviction that *this* day you'll finally be content,
that only tears of victory will be spent.

Scars from a Mugging

The past encroaches on the here and now
and unwelcome recall reminds you how its feels
to be forced to bow
down before the threat of unyielding steel.

Who would not be shaken
by that traitorous moment in time
when almost everything you prize is taken?

What is worse, I want to ask, *the crime
or how it is remembered?*

Memory assaults me with remorseless hits,
anguish ruthlessly tendered
as counterweight to my fault; a penalty that squarely fits
my crime. Later - having paid the requisite fee -
recovery from my abandonment of you will be solely down to me.

The Hunt for Meaning in Experience

Some mythologies are esteemed
while others languish, being
dangerous and dark. Wisdom is deemed
the reward of years, of seeing
falsehoods for what they are. Our tired eyes
shot through with blood
habitually search the gloom for spies
who would deny the prize of all that's good.
In a pre-dawn's level
light, some beliefs we own
plead for prominence on life's bevel
and - thus raised - hope to show
how we might yet maintain
the fight, allow experience to reign.

Check-up

When the doctors scanned my brain
were they scavenging for memory,
connections that retain
links to the past, the empty rest… eternity?

When the doctors examined my heart
was it to define whether love exists
woven in the fabric of the mechanical part
or there in an x-ray's shadow previously missed?

When the doctors begged me to hold
on longer, unforgiving time kept score
in numbers etched in bold
on bed-framed notes. I had expected more;
something definitive to solve the mystery
of why my life looked this way to me.

On revisiting an old home now derelict

Unprepared for change
surely my sudden surprise might
have been forgiven for finding strange
these crumbled walls when they came into sight.
In this house there had been much to admire.
And though its fabric is grown old
it still seeds in me a desire
for bed-time fables, to be told
stories of those who defied
the ravages of the past,
turned history to a lie.
Might these legends allow me to make haste
and imagine how it used to be
living in that old house and being a younger version of me?

Industrial Unrest

Never consciously against the state
his principles were fathered
when a friend died, betrayed by commercial haste.

Later they gathered
galvanised by accident
and the way objection falls
on deaf ears. Their crescendo of discontent
became a drumbeat call
for change. Was he a heretic
in pleading for humane working hours?

His words, made falsely politic
by those who weaponised his call for showers
or safety gear, played to the pulse of time
and encouraged the Establishment to translate protest into crime.

The Manifesto of the Soul

It shuffles restlessly under a canopy
of skin, pretence in its honouring
of love or the con-trick of eternity.
Duplicity and veiled double-talk is ruining
the naïve, like an old best friend seeking favour
to help settle unpaid rent.
Your reward? The chance to savour
its illusory depth, seduced by quality-time spent
in a brittle alliance with the heart.

All it wants is to be free.

Skeleton keys masquerade as art
as it picks at locks so deftly.
It's searching for a manifesto, this soul
over which we've no control.

The Terror of Clock Chimes

We think we hold them in our power
and dally with each bewitched hour
as if starring in a one-man show
or absurdly in control of what we know.
On time's intemperate rack
ligaments tense and bring us back
to memories of half-perfected skill
and those days we strived to kill
with meaningless pleasure
or fruitless search for buried treasure.

Bereft of a manual telling us how to be
blindly we chime towards an unmapped country.

Slave Trader

It was an honour you judged fair
the bequeathing of your surname.
Not qualified as heirs
it hung around necks a badge of shame,
proof of your power.

Later - or too late - how might you have saved face
rather than retreat into the bower
of bequeathed history, head hung in disgrace,
wary of the black
and thunderous clouds that seemed
ready to rebel against lack
of freedom? Trapped in a perpetuating web of self-esteem
you were woven from the fabric of others' woe
and knitted into history forever so.

A Game of Chance

We listen to the DJ play
anonymous sounds
bound to make us sway
until their rhythm confounds
our senses, gives permission to leap
caution's chasm hand-in-hand,
liberates us to later reap
the debris of a one-night-stand.

Chance inhabits every altered state
like the scattering of poker chips
on life's baize - or that nervous gait
across the bedroom floor to waiting lips
as if 'love', camouflaged amidst all of this,
might be unwrapped by that first impassioned kiss.

Descent thru' Virtue and Vice

Duels are fought: pride wrestling shame;
love versus lust;
responsibility battling blame.
Abdicating decisions to trust,
we set our course straight
toward the epic, to mimic those who had
the wit to circumvent the bait
which made many others mad.

Was it ever so
being tortured by extreme
experiences of woe?

On our descent from dream
we trudge through Dante's well
to one day knock at the welcoming gates of hell.

Seashore Sunset

The swiftly declining sun
paints narrow strips of cloud smokey red,
leaves fields brushed the softest dun,
and remarkable at the peninsula's head
the still untainted chalky white
of imperious cliffs. And I recall your cheeks
still pink with delight
from post-noon beach scrambles, how seaweed reeks
when abandoned by the tide, how we instinctively know
the rhythms in the sound
of waves as they come and go
pawing at this frontier ground.
Such composition is so rare,
a multicoloured landscape beyond compare.

5-right; 58-left

They say safe-cracking's an art,
an addiction to the cruel
and taunting click at the heart
of cold machinery. And all for a jewel
you're told is priceless to behold.

Your fingers slip; you groan
at the fumbling. Feeling less than bold
crouching in the darkness alone
ineptitude makes you swear
aloud, and on your sweat-stained face
tell-tale signs that you cannot bear
the cocooned quiet of this haunted place,
knowing traitors witness your illicit deeds
awaiting their moment to indulge their vicious greed.

Mourning Clothes

After you abandoned me
some other-worldly disdain
demanded to know how it was to be
without you. I asked how much pain
was requisite as entrance fee for heaven.

Hearing rumours of salvation, I headed east
searching unceasingly - even
far enough for east to blend back to west.
Dissembling self-assurance to save face
I sought gaffer tape for a fragile heart,
mimicked good emotional posture to maintain grace
enough to play my now one-handed and unscripted part.

Returning to an empty home the world looks black,
discoloured by the knowledge of what I lack.

One more day in Confinement

Rusted hinges groan.
The reinforced door shuts against me.
I feel again what it is to be alone,
imagine a world where to be
solitary is never taken
for granted. In isolation I'm engrossed
in remembrance of past joys forsaken;
keep my fingers crossed
those footsteps coming down the ward
will be the dream of psychological bail
made real; that my erstwhile guard
will jangle his keys to this unforgiving jail,
choose to smile benevolently
and finally open the door for me.

Song of the Abused

Less tuneful than a high-pitched whine
my song's misshapen by your will.
In darkest shadow some thing of mine
cowers, holding tightly still
to the mirage of liberty.

Sometimes I would imagine you kind,
that you hadn't beaten me,
my flesh no longer raw from your habit to bind
too tightly and for the smallest mistake.

Imagination, I'd think, what's the use?
Don't fret for my sake.
It's not pain but psychological abuse
that most tortures me
and fuels my desperate longing to be free.

The Beneficiary

after Louis D'Ascoyne

Now in possession of the keys he will
find a use for the surplus
furniture, tell himself the outcome was still
worth the painful legal fuss.
He has been gifted spacious
rooms, stairs made serpentine
by twisting newell posts and gracious
balustrades; the paintwork shines
as if the decorators were in there still.
What else might be in store?

What do they say: *where there's a way there's a will?*
From unlocked attic rooms the promise of more
drowns out the voice reminding him he'd had to kill
to get his hands on a suitably rewarding will.

Waiting for a train, nervously

The panel lies that the train is near
- as if LEDs had sufficient will
to propel one even faster here.
Catching it will be a promise I fulfil,
embarking on a quest to demonstrate my love.

Under the awning on platform one
I wonder if that's all I have to prove.

Seeking answers, I hear none
above the metronomic announcer's retold
rules: he tells me where to stand, who to be,
he warns me to hold
my baggage close as if in jeopardy.

Previous failures reside in memory still,
each echo the weakening of my already fragile will.

Catch, landed

There are words in your eyes.
Etched along the lines of your lashes I see
the mascara of lies.
Who knew honesty could be
inferior to good looks,
common sense taken for a ride?

I nibble at all your baited hooks,
am teased by feathery lures perfectly tied.
I tell myself this is not a plot
rather an unhappy circumstance of place,
and in falling for your well-cast words - not
heeding truths escaping from the keep-net of your face -
I find my life is now interred,
drowning in air, my will to you transferred.

Young and Old Revolutionaries in Conversation

So what is truth?
The opposite of lies
- though you in your youth
will miss its subtleties.

Do you remember being young?
Every day. It was the best
thing to be, revolution always on the tongue.

Yet you were suppressed,
forced to heel by the unjust.
And now I am old.

Will you place me in your trust?
I wonder… Will you do what you are told
or end up just like me,
pining for youth - not freedom - and how it was to be?

Testimony of a War Artist

They all stop short of saying that it's wrong,
this inner battle between head and heart
and which gains sovereignty over tongue.

Though not appreciating art
they take me for what I am. Kept in their sight
with surprising gentleness they ease me to one side,
protect me as best they might,
suggest I keep my head down. *Bide
your time* they say, *who knows
what tricks our enemies
might play?* We pretend our foes
never succumb to the self-same injuries
as we, or are never slain,
or, being evil, that they deserve their pain.

Opening the Bowling

The captain will tell us it's the time to press,
unafraid to show his distain
for the opposition. He will express
defeat as the infliction of a pain
impossible to bear, as if - were
we to lose - we'd all be damned. And so
he'll ask Silly Point to field too near
- pretending he doesn't know
to do so Jack will need to be as mad
or as possessed as he.

Later, nerves leaving me having never felt so bad,
I begin my run-up hoping to be
more than good, my skill not belied
- then bowl my first delivery far too wide.

Bitter Harvest

They say laughter's in the eyes
and friendship's carried by a note
in the voice. Does their absence suggest I despise
you as equally as you seem to dote
on me? Or be unreasonably delighted
to leave you emotionally prone
when finding you're not invited
to my soirée? How *do* you cope alone?

Yet a softer voice asks me how I can
bear to see you in such misery;
protests that there's another man
- and a better one - to be;
asks what it is I really gain
to seed in you such a crop of pain.

Second Among Equals

Trespassing a fine line, my younger brother's hate
for me is resolute; he assumes I'm loving
the largesse of my newly inherited estate.
Bitter prejudice is reproving
of first editions, rare wine,
fine-china mantle ornaments
which unsought are now all mine.
He rails against taxes, rents
and bills as if responsibility for those
must now reside with me.

Daily I watch his jaundice grow.

Is there no other self for him to be
but the embodiment of what he cannot hide,
fury at some moral justice unreasonably denied?

The Great Escape

Steve allows the clutch to catch
and accelerates away
leaping rolling terrain, aiming to dispatch
the barbed-wire bonds which prolong his stay.
Bike-mounted guards give chase,
pursue the Cooler King hell-bent
until he slides defeated to the turf; on his face
months of accumulated discontent.

Is this intoxicating fantasy
or do we all have something we wish to leave behind?

If so, what does that purport for me?
Might the future prove more kind,
accept the inclination of my will
and, cameras rolling, see my ride to freedom continued still?

Treasure Island

There is something subterranean about despair
where surrendered once means surrendered still.

Divorced from all we might consider fair
the pirate within means us ill,
sponsors this skin-deep dig for evil
knowing what's there, who's on his side
and already contracted to the devil.

When he's not looking, we pan for pride
hoping it doesn't prove the fiend
we fear; that we'll uncover life-raft stories to tell
and one day recount those to a friend,
glory in the mythology of our escape from hell.

There can be no entertaining doubt,
so we'll persist and sift that treasure out!

At the Un-fun Fair

Why did you always make
me go on rides you knew I'd hate?
It was never for my own sake.
You'd revel in my unravelled state,
yet plead with me to come
with you on the Waltzer, sweet-
talk me from premonitions of Rollercoaster doom.
Each new scare you'd greet
with unconstrained joy, and
eventually boast of the completeness of your day.
At times like that you were a fiend
I wished might be tossed away
as lightly as those plastic darts I threw
always hoping to win the prize of you.

Fracking Greed

Concrete resembles the earth.
Overhead an invisible telescopic array
predicts the continuing dearth
of water. There is nothing gay
in forecasting our lease
is running out, that no mega-spend
will counter the previous excess
now pointing toward a devastating end.
Smooth-talkers never mentioned loss;
how could our bounteous store
one day shrink to dust and dross?
Yet still they would squeeze out more
these be-suited neolithic men -
and after that, what then?

Residue from an Argument

The morning dawns uncertain still
clouded by memory of the malevolent disease
which yesterday manifested only ill.
Why did you ignore my pleas
to remember what love
once was, the vows which should have kept
us bound? Do you still approve
of what you yelled, accept
you strayed from mutual care,
played your part in sourcing that unrest?
Our earlier selves aren't what we're
now become; how we felt back then is not expressed
by anger. If only today might beckon bright
after the trauma of such a conflicted night.

As the Incompetents hog the Stage
(in response to yet another UK PM being sworn in)

The carousel brings confusion to my head,
its lights and spinning faces blurring sight.
To save itself, Common Sense has fled
in trails of smoke - truth's bonfire now alight -
and witless onlookers dote
on soundbites in the vacuum. And so
one loses all sense of how to denote
the real from what's not. No
syllable in the Ring Masters' address remains true,
happiness and grief a confusion of tears.

Is it wrong to seek a better view,
to hope that later, as sight clears,
I'll discover we're not all blind
and a crumb of political salvation find?

After I won the Lottery

Once you were a person not
needing bribery to partake
in building history - old experiences now forgot
for self-salvation's sake.
Can I still call you friend
or does that rest upon
some new and graduated spend
to inhibit an all too eager moan
prompted by fiscal disrespect?
How can you despise
me for what's not a true defect?
Financial envy occludes your eyes
and constantly brings to mind
this new imbalance which leaves you twisted, blind.

Over-reaction to a Ill-timed Accusation

Some base untempered ore I might
try to melt with words if that would sway
this unwanted outcome. Has sight
ever witnessed a more gun-metal day?

You decided my intentions were for ill,
ineptitude in execution of deeds
evidenced the crudeness of skills
now proven not to exceed
misplaced confidence. If I had shown more
care, how much shallower would your hate
be now? Other excuses would be needed to abhor
me as you do. Emotional exile, my present state,
is punishment reflecting poorly on me -
as does your response to my unintended calumny.

The Friar Protests

The two of them expect me to understand this
vapour they're so keen to label 'love'.
Yet why argue something tribal is amiss
simply to offer fault against which to prove
supremacy of this 'softer' passion? Would you still betray
your kin if love was a treason
punishable by death? I'd hoped - the acts played out - you may
have gained the wisdom to promote reason
beyond that you *think* you see.
Your parents plea for less love, more pride;
argue it's enough to be
enriched by the familial side.
Even so, I suspect you'll choose to make a call
that will lead to an inevitable and tragic fall.

Blind Loyalty

Is there nothing they might have sworn
to satisfy you, and in so swearing
found a way for the world not to be torn
asunder? Always cowed by your bearing
down on them, swamped by your majesty,
they struggled more than most
to articulate paternal loyalty.

And now everything is lost.
A sham of kindness
reigns; empty soundbites pretending constancy
echo from castle walls. Even in my blindness
I know these for mere vapours. Can you not see?
Surely you need not even one eye
to understand the treason behind a lie.

Bottom's Bully-boy

The nincompoop's asleep!
And he wasn't the only one I found
bumbling about the make-shift stage near the steep
slope up to the Pleasure Ground.
Snoring, I bet he dreams of Love!

Mythology tells them it will endure,
triumph over those who prove
diabolical. But Love is no cure
for ignorance! That idiot may be fired-
up, contented in his puffed-up breast,
imagine himself most handsome, most desired.
Yet Love is a mind's unruly guest
keeping its distance with sugary lies
and all that rubbish about soul-finding in the eyes.

Dreaming of Daggers

I did not expect to find her asleep
like this, her peppery brand
of energy doused. Tomorrow she will keep
me to the task, her spotless hands
helping stoke the fire.
More passion- than duty-warmed
is the infection of her desire
even if I long to be disarmed
by something softer. Set on edge by
nightmares of damnation's perpetual
agonies, I know there is no remedy,
no way to escape her thrall,
nothing I have left to prove
other than the execution of my love.

Acknowledgements

Reference material:
- *The Sonnets*, William Shakespeare; Signet Classic (The New American Library of World Literature Inc.), 1965
- *W. H. Auden, Collected Poems*, W. H. Auden, Faber and Faber, 1994
- *After the Rehearsals*, Ian Gouge, Coverstory books, 2018

Previous publications:
- a version of "Pilgrimage" was first published in the online edition of *The Aesthetic Apostle*, February 2019, and then later in *The Myth of Native Trees*, Coverstory books, 2020, and *Selected Poems: 1976-2022*, Coverstory books, 2022
- earlier versions of "After the Threshing" (as "The Seasons"), "In Mourning", "Orienteering", "Late Frost", and "Slam, Vulnerable" were first published in *The Myth of Native Trees*, Coverstory books, 2020. "In Mourning" was also later published in *Selected Poems: 1976-2022*, Coverstory books, 2022

www.ingramcontent.com/pod-product-compliance
Lightning Source LLC
Chambersburg PA
CBHW021106080526
44587CB00010B/403

9781739766030